CONSOLAT

ROY FULLER

Consolations

SECKER & WARBURG
LONDON

First published in England 1987 by
Martin Secker & Warburg Limited
54 Poland Street, London WIV 3DF

Reprinted 1987

British Library Cataloguing in Publication Data

Fuller, Roy
Consolations.
I. Title
821'.912   PR6011.U55

ISBN 0–436–16791–3

Typeset by Inforum Ltd, Portsmouth
Printed in England by
Redwood Burn Ltd, Trowbridge

Let no smalnesse retard thee; if thou beest not a Cedar to help towards a palace, if thou beest not Amber, Bezoar, nor liquid gold, to restore Princes; yet thou art a shrub to shelter a lambe, or to feed a bird; or thou art a plantane, to ease a child's smart; or a grasse to cure a sick dog.

John Donne: *Essays in Divinity* (quoted in Helen Gardner's *In Defence of the Imagination*)

CONTENTS

I

Age

DOWN KAUNDA STREET

Kenya revisited after forty years!
But only in Nina Casimati's *Guide*.

Why didn't I view more the Kenyan part
Of the 'vast fault' that deeply wounds the earth
Between the Siberian lake and great Zimbabwe?

It seems Nairobi has dual carriage-ways –
Maybe the road that led in former days
From the camp to Lady Delamere's canteen;
The road one travelled standing up in trucks,
Across the Senecan night-time of the plain.

I fail to impose on my shapeless memories
The rigour of the city's Yankee grid.
Besides, most names are novel: I may well
Have been shampoo'd by the Asian Sweeney Todd
In what's now Banda or Kaunda Street.
But even then the future could be divined –
The empire's break-up – more through our tender hearts
Than contemplating military defeat.

Despite its being exile, I came to love
The strange land. The vocabulary of
Swahili given here brings back emotions
Perhaps I never truly owned again.
In retrospect, quite startling I was then
So intimately interlocked with humans
And malevolent devices that could hurt.

[3]

What friendships torn in two, myself quite blind
To anything (when at last the moment came)
Save the long voyage to the *patria*!
– Where now the commonalty's going up in flames . . .
Lit by dark citizens of Rome, their names
Half Latin, who never clapped eyes on Africa.

Kwaheri Kenya, 'cradle of mankind'!

QUESTIONS OF ENTROPY

A few grave questions rise still. Shall I ever
Possess a soldering-iron of my own?
Is it next door a true or false acacia?

I soldered (not soldiered) in the War, was never
A proletarian before. Unknown
Most trees to me, townee, as desert Asia.

Thank God a lot of fellows write in prose –
I think in the middle of the night, when verse
Would be a quite too gagging brew to absorb;

And might bring queries I try not to pose,
Such as how every night makes matter worse,
Despite the mensual splendour of the orb.

AT THE IMPERIAL WAR MUSEUM

To Catherine Reilly

Occasion really more for prose than verse,
A Proustian or Powellian gathering,
The 9th November 1984:
Amazing little poetry-reading at
The Imperial War Museum – women poets
Of World War II – with plonk served afterwards.
The background: that paradox, the marvellous art
Produced in wartime; the rambling building in
The Lambeth Road one somehow never fathoms
(The former Bedlam, rather appropriately),
Behind the naval guns one never fired.
The audience largely the poets and their friends,
I guess. Good grief, survivors of that war,
So recent as it seems, now tend towards
The decrepit. Yet some still astonish with
Remnants of youth, the beauty we used to say
A sad goodbye to in those rotten days.
I'm told a few are dead I really feel
Are still alive; although I more and more,
Reading of deaths, forget, and resurrect
A dead one in my brain. The book back of
The recital, I peruse, plonk-softened, in
The bus that takes me home along the once
Bomb-fractured Old Kent Road, and so return
The names and phrases half-forgotten since
My wartime years. I think what myriad
Lovers and chums and verse those years threw up;
Perverse as ever, showings of the human.
Great girls, who wept for England and for us;
Meriting more than blank pentameters –
Muted Elgarian trombones at least.

EMPEROR'S TOMB FOUND IN CHINA

Six servants had been sacrificed
To prepare the ghostly meal – an era before
Effigies came to replace the slain retainers.

Deep in the attic of a kitchen cupboard
A pile of plates is found, by time embrowned,
Though not concealing gilt and dark-blue rims.

What epoch of our lives were they in use?
Plainly before the Ravilious by Wedgwood:
But how could they precede the 'modernist'

Pastel-green wedding-present dinner-service?
My mother must have passed them down when I
Started a home and she relinquished hers.

And so perhaps it's filial guilt prevents
My now remembering them; although today
Memory and unmemory both seem whims.

Among my infancy's mills and moors, my mother
Girlish, what ghostly meals were served on those
Platters, by servants dead as in old Cathay!

Note: The title and some phrases from Norman Hammond, archaeology correspondent of *The Times* (20 August, 1985), with gratitude.

FIVE-FINGER EXERCISE

'I want a sketch book bound in human skin
To write some of the things I am doing now' –
One can't but envy the Elgarian
Hyperbole. Still, almost everyone
Of any talent at that astounding time
Of dreaming Freud and dug-up Troy might well
Have aimed to mark his *oeuvre nobilmente*.

And so another meditation starts.
The upper trunks of the acacia trees
Resemble pythons. Are simple likenesses
Still to be set down, after a life of such?
It seems inherent in the art, and yet
One wants to write the monarch's funeral march;
Invent a tune and then transfigure it.

More dubious sides of creativity
Exist – in Elgar's day, and even now:
The tenor attitude, one foot withdrawn.
Who can be sure he isn't posturing?
Scriabin hurt his hand through practising
Too much in youth, quite probably his own
Digit-destroying work. Now that's all right.

BORN 1912

I

In such works as the tedious diaries
Of Beatrice Webb I come across accounts
Of that summer of strikes, the tropical summer
Of 1911 – as strange as 1912's
Moroccan crisis, when the great powers rehearsed
What in my infancy and youth I called
The Great War. All the years my parents knew
Of thrift and modesty and sensible art
Began to be cancelled.
                        Now long other years
Have passed, and miraculously I'm still here;
And writing in comprehensible iambics;
And bringing in the common things of life –
A pigeon jumping down a step, and landing
On both feet, like an infant. Though I feel
My age prevents my taking up the cheap
And shameless offer in the green-grocer's shop
By some permissive, self-styled 'loose bananas'.

II

I ponder on a colleague's deep enquiry
About my health. For, after all, he's new;
Don't know him well. Am I then thin and pine
After the illness I've taken more or less
In my stride, or is he simply manifesting
The human virtue old age tends to make
Old age forget?
                I come home from the meeting
And hear 'The Planets' on the radio –
Astounding and daring work, though scarcely younger
Than I, apparently so close to death.

III

D major: 'Most resonant of string keys.' So
I read; somewhat mysterious words to one
Quite ignorant of musical technique.
The phrase applies to a Mendelssohn quartet –
Composer still not wholly unmaligned
After a century and a half. That keys
Still enter into aesthetic consciousness,
One renders faintly unbelieving thanks.
Just as I journey a mere hundred yards
To shop, and return with poetic images –
For instance, a neighbour lost in thought before
A supermarket shelf, her beauty changed
(Time infiltrating through relaxed defences)
To the uncertainties of middle-age;
Nevertheless, an age not knowing war,
An age when I was safely in the womb.

HEARTS AND FLOWERS

Ancient tragedy's dish of mad revenge –
Preparing hearts for the table. Is this all?
So simple – a mass of meat, a tube, with fat
Adhering, quite unharmful in adolescent
Breasts (from whose woolly whiteness these were drawn).
Experience tells one they'll be tough; then how
Came some such organs to class themselves as tender?
I'm touched, but scarcely with compassion eating
My heart out: too removed from murderers
My meagre pence per pound ignobly hired.

The robin gives his wife a notable grub.
Or she gives him – if plumage be the sole
Criterion, ambiguous in their kind.

Obeying wiser gardeners, I shower
A foliar feed on beheaded daffodils;
Although to see again a sudden gold
Conquer the frost seems as remote as settling
The right speeds of the Goldberg variations.

But what indeed will rest on the turntable
At my demise? What part-played work, perhaps
The lowest common multiple of my taste,
Will they lift up, throw out with other junk?
– When that crude thing of protein and grease has failed,
Its modest share of selfless love descending
To generations that will little know
It also trafficked with acherontic powers.

A SORT OF ART

'manufactured here in Crete' – *from the back of an envelope*

Merely announcement of intention
May constitute a sort of art:
'Next year . . .' 'I want . . .' 'I'll touch your heart.'

To usher on the stage a Prologue,
Then have him heckled by a huge
Lout from the pit, or other stooge;

To start – indeed, never end – a fable:
'It turned out that a goose-girl . . .' 'Once
Upon a time three questing sons . . .'

But pusillanimous, unthorough
Such things, whatever a lenient age
May sanction on the stage or page,

Allowing prosy authors phrases,
Mysterious or incomplete
(Like 'manufactured here in Crete'),

That in some volume now forgotten
Captured their fancy at a time
When sheer bosh might go into rhyme.

And writing this, I still sit wearing
My kitchen apron, Pasternak
On the chair-arm, and at my back

Ice-dominated climates, loony
Dictators, that I've so far dodged
Though in their histories firmly lodged

– Detergent draining from our English
Pots that like me remain to be
Cracked in some frightful destiny.

[12]

CURRYING FAVOUR

I feed initially suspicious dogs
(Tied up outside the supermarket store)
With 'Good Boy' vitaminized chocolate drops.
A pleasure of old age is to confer
A wholly unexpected benefit:
Reason: unclear. It's surely not the sense,
Retained from indoctrination when a child,
Of the approach, near death, of Judgement Day.
Besides, in almost every other way
Old age is famous for its selfishness;
And it may well be, having lost one's looks,
One tries to get in even dogs' good books.

THE SCALE

How near the human, the animal!
How much nearer, the senile or insane!

The cat chatters at me as I defend
The birds whose bright eyes recognize

But little approve of me, like girls.
Are we a caricature, we old,

Of the human; or truly human? A few
Years, perhaps, before one descends the scale.

OLD LADIES AND GENTLEMEN

Occasional result of adolescent
Anorexia: 'eccentric wizened old ladies'

– Or so I read: a novelistic fate.
But what seized us in our youth, we ancient men?

WRITING AND DRINKING

Little the earliest chemists of root and grain
Considered it was really for the Muse
They conjured bubbles, droplets clear as rain
– Or so I think, composing poems few
Will ever repeat, in years when man may well
Revert to brutish societies pre-booze.
Each sip I take is a libation to
Science and art, once fused, ruled by a girl.

THE AMBIGUOUS MUSHROOM

I make to kick a mushroom in the lane;
At the last moment wisely withdraw my shoe,
Seeing the object is in fact a turd,
Dropped by a fox, perhaps, or rather more
Appropriate in the comic context, the
Uncommon shaping by a common cur.
It happened I was musing on the liking
That human beings seem to have in art
For the maniacal; say, the later Blake
Or, with all due respect, Karlheinz Stockhausen
(Whose music moves from one imperfectly
Tuned wavelength to another of the same).
What does the versing from excrement portend?
It may to some appear a paradox
That one is not about to prophesy,
Nor specify glissandos of loud farts.

HOMAGE TO JAROSLAV SEIFERT

Only by the long lashes
Of the profile in front
Do I know it's not a lad
Eating the meat pasty.

I myself am devouring
Jaroslav Seifert's verse –
Just to the astonishment of most
Awarded a Nobel prize.

Written at seventy-nine,
Giving me seven years, this book
Even in translation whacks my own
Transcriptions of the past.

Why shouldn't London stun like Prague?
It does; and memories of skin
And fragrancies could match the Czech's,
If told with equal craft.

The 53 glances off
Parliament Square, and leaves behind
Statues and devious rulers, bound
For my study's suburban heights.

Should I survive as long as Seifert,
The meat-pie eater may
Become in time a song in some
Nostalgia-conjuring metre.

PROGRESS

A neighbour complains the local fox tears open
The plastic bags the Council have supplied
To help the poor old dustmen by compelling
People to take their trash to their front gates.
But she departs before I think to say:
Preferable to a lamb's soft underside.

II

Footnotes

TOUCHING

'Ne me touchez pas, ne me touchez pas!'
– Mélisande, *très* womanly.
Still to come, the truly disastrous
Results of touching. And finally,
Eager obedience
To that feminine command.

ON FIRST LOOKING INTO THE PENGUIN BOOK OF GREEK VERSE

Thracian filly, why do you cruelly
Avoid me? On plains where the naked girls
Wake harvesting clover with their light yellow arms,
A drowned noise lingers as from the twang of a bow –
The bowman who was afflicted by his wound?

Get three small grey-fish and two dozen humped
Prawns, and send Chryseis of the beautiful cheeks.
A little old woman will hold our hand and tell us,
Pale-faced, of the bitterness of life, as if
It were a fairy tale, the nightingale greeting the dawn
With laments for Itys, daylight but a finger.

What was the greatest wish of my mad heart?
Fill the cup and say again, again, again:
'To Heliodora.' Strange drinking party! –
Leaves large as the footprint of a crow;
The swallows a black string of dancers;
And the black dress gathers round her navel.
But who ever got to the distant Island of Joy?

Another city shall be found, better
Than this – its splendid colts, its great sea-power.
And the girls of our village will be standing round us
In the dream of the sea and of the sky.

Do not lament your luck, your work that has failed:
Great Pan is not dead, no, great Pan does not die.

Note: The poem is composed of phrases from the 'plain prose transla-
tions' by the editor of the anthology, Constantine A. Trypanis, to
whom apologies and thanks.

AN OLD STORY

'Child, whatever ails thee?
– Inward eye and cheek.
Seems as though life fails thee.
Durst not speak?

'Pale, albeit surely
Stouter than heretofore:
Living, oh so purely,
What wouldst more?'

'Mother, greying, worried –
How can I reply?
Even in times far buried
Tha felt not as I.'

'Child how vast thine error.
Though unborn when
I crept about in terror,
Tha wert in being then.'

BOOLOO

I

The islands of that ocean are dispersed
As planets, likewise capturing the sun
Among a vacancy of deepest blue.

Some are mere asteroids: such I landed on.
Landed! – a cutter from the plying ship
Dumped me at a rotting landing-stage.

A choice of three guest-houses, as I'd heard.
Since Charley's droshky was already by
The quay, I went to Charley's 'Number Two' –

Though later found that Sula's put on three
Good meals a day. However, soon I moved
Into a rented 'deteriorating cottage' –

Phrase almost euphemistic what with bats
And rats; and above the ground-bass of the rain
Drippings playing various tunes in tins.

'Doing a minor Gauguin,' so they said.
One felt more a convict or a mutineer;
At best dependent on the shipping-line's

Profit and loss account, or even whim,
Or the world's taste for coconuts and such,
To get back to the life one had renounced.

Still, over drink, a man might tell you when
They sailed in with the novelty of axes;
Times before girls had necklaces of beads.

Kava, the local tipple, but narcotic
Rather than alcoholic: numb effect
Of the dentistry I bravely left behind.

The colour of dark chocolate, Kava, quite
Gratuitously nasty, so no wonder
I quickly contemplated other vices.

[22]

I used to sit in trousers in the wavelets
(That made once-grubby toe-nails pink as shells)
To cool off, sober up, while congregated

The solemn or grinning children of the isle.
And soon I hired my twelve-year-old, and was
Domesticated as in times gone by.

Uxorious – long hair, with sea-flowers crowned!
And even fewer words to hold my mind
Than bourgeois girls had uttered in the north.

She thought my dollars counters in some game.
Well, this was usually the view of more
Sophisticated follies of my past.

But was it the linguistic barrier,
Or poverty, or skin that made me think
I could as negligently return with her

As with a Gyppo valet or Chinese cook?
To what? Suburban stuffiness, looking out
Over the city's illuminated hills

To where a kind of other life goes on
In talkative cafés, with booze no more
Consolatory for being subtly hued.

– The stoic poet once again; perhaps
An even greater failure, certainly
At monstrous risk in amatory affairs.

Only too late I saw how happy she
Had been after I'd bought her in the isle;
Status assured, the 'cottage' above her station.

II

She soon expired. The civilized microbes were
Impossible to fight. In her native land
The highest rank alone have souls, and so

She may have never travelled more. And, since
The corner where her sepia remains

[23]

Were buried now is utterly overgrown,

Often it seems mere fantasy (as though
The bodying out of my neuroses) that
She ever lived, and here. I might have caused

Her name to be cut into churchyard stone
Had I been sure of it. 'Booloo' I called her,
But that was just half their word for drawing up

A dress, to cover modestly the shoulders,
And meant in that form any adhesive stuff.
Poor, dear Booloo, how well you stuck to me,

Except when proving your people's idea of death –
The intervention of an evil spirit.
At that long drawn-out time I couldn't help

Recalling when was washed up on the shore
A whale long-dead, the stench so terrible
Only the lowest-born would venture close

To cut out the numerous and precious teeth.
Yet you could be concerned about Bulotu,
The now distant island Kingdom of the Dead –

An island like that ocean's other isles,
But where no solid food is needed, merely
Shadow-food (already apt for you).

Its air, just as deliciously perfumed
As whaleless island shores, is nonetheless
The air of Death, unfitted for mortal lungs . . .

And so that smudge of smoke's abstruse emotion,
When S.S. *Dugong* returned at last to exchange
Its trashy novelties for your devotion,

Turned out to be unhappiness – for me
At least: your voyage, marriage, house of stone,
Assured (you told me) your status for Bulotu;

Only remained to find some craft to take you.

THE MARCELLUS VERSION

With thanks to James Fenton

Pass me the water. Yes, I played Marcellus.
You'd think I'd not at my age want to cut
The wine, but life seems something now to cherish,
Having survived its sotted years, and roles
Even more dim and ill-paid than Marcellus.
'To be or not to be?' Eh? There's the point.
'To die, to sleep, is *that* all?' There it goes.
You get the answer simply by surviving.
There's nothing after death, not even dreams.
But life's worth living. Yes, despite the fact
That wives die far too early or too late;
And rotten luck; and botched ambition.

It must be twenty years ago he came
And asked me what I remembered of the play.
Nick Lang or Ling his name; and then a dog
Called Sims, black-fingered printer from the City,
Took down my words. Odd's blood, the longest sessions
Of canting and Canary ever known!
I'd been a quick study, quick also to forget.
Whether the fellows knew this, who can tell?
Or why they lit on me. There was a haste
To be the first to sell it to the gulls
And play it in the provinces. Quoth I:
'What part for me?' 'Marcellus.' 'Goblin damned!'
'Also the doubling in the pantomime.'
I took the ducats for my memory
And let them toil to Preston with the play.
I stayed in town. Worked, yes, but rested more.

Anon I met old Whatshisname in Southwark –
Who'd played Corambis on that very tour –
Complaining of a cropped and mangled script,
Not knowing (what a hoot!) the text was mine,
Nor thankful for a part so full of juice,
And lodging in great houses with all found.
He claimed the play had been new printed – twice
The length of my dredged-up memories (the liar) –

And with the ancient hight Polonius,
A part he well might never play again
Since he was, as t'were, for ever Corambis.
Seems Ling and Co had got the bard's foul papers
(Lost at the time the villains came to me)
And set the whole boiling. Proliferating fumes
Of the sack-soaked lunatic poet in his study!

But all that was before the interim
In which babes turned to heroines. My son
(Dead Susan's child) once played Marcellus, and
The servant to Coram – Polonius.
And now you've lugged along a new-born whale
(Anyway, darling, broad-backed like a whale) –
A folio of plays, and all (it seems)
By Shakeshaft. How this would have astounded him,
Who loved the book-trade rather less than I.
And your inserted digit marks a place:
'To be or not to be, that is the question.'
Aye. Well. I see. The poet makes his points.
But note, the length is not much more than mine.
In Preston or, indeed, the City they'd
Have hissed the author's original traffic, yawned
At the coiling of his sub-plot.

                    Bloody cold,
He made it feel on the battlements, admitted.
And by-the-by, even in mid-career
He didn't always get the ictus right.
Give me the tome again. Look here, for instance:
'Touching this dreaded sight twice seen of us.'
Somehow you've got to stress the 'twice' and 'us'
To bring the sense home; yet speak trippingly.
What's left i' the jug? No, no, the wine, the wine.

LITERARY FOOTNOTES

Fame

I found, encountering her in Drury Lane,
Mrs Centlivre had become a pain
In the neck; and less because of any book
Than having late in life wed Queen Anne's cook.

She was extremely actressy and grand;
Her speech and bosom reached down to the Strand.
Our talk, though, was not of entrances and wigs
But recipes for roasting sucking-pigs.

I prophesy that in the future doubt
Must drench what's said (if anything) about
Susannah's plays; that her enduring fame
Will be through ending with a curious name.

Two American Poets

Adelaide Crapsey, Amy Clampitt –
You've got to accept the names or lump it.
Amy Clampitt, Adelaide Crapsey –
Which the sobersides, which the wild gypsy?

Felicity

Feeling the felicity of being
At once part of and passenger through
The universe, I wonder how
To capture that second of deep seeing.

And can't help grinning at the far
Image that rises in my sane
But excessively literary brain:
Driving in Edith Wharton's car.

STRANGE REVELATIONS

To Louis Allen

What energy I had not long ago
To go to Durham to spout my poetry!
I doubt wild horses – even, Louis, you –
Could drag me there today.

It was then I exhausted my surprise (though not
My admiration) on discovering
Your oriental learning – you a French don
In the ordinary way.

So not quite unexpected finding you
Reviewing in the *TLS* two books
Of tales and poem-tales from 'old Japan'
(As thus they used to say).

I've always longed to write mysterious works,
Though conscience, as a rule, compelling me
To stick to life, my life, and so express
Mostly the everyday.

– Therefore read enviously of 'endless puns'
In classic Japanese; the puzzling titles;
Uncovering of a strange reality
Beneath the common clay.

The 'Minor Captain' shelters from the rain,
Sees through her rattan blinds a long-haired girl,
Answers her singing with a verse – and spends
The night with her. Next day

She gets from him a gift, a 'dish of greens',
Accompanied by further poetry,
This time inscribed (but who knows how?) upon
Plum-blossom's blanched display.

Many years afterwards the warrior,
Become a Buddhist monk, conveys to her
His washing, presumably exiguous . . .
These things seem quite outré.

But offering her his subfusc 'robe of hemp'
Can also mean 'I lie prone, sleep alone.'
In this art even laundry-lists may read
    With ambiguous overlay.

Elsewhere: 'the supernatural invades
The secular . . . The world of animals
Blends with the world of men.' Enigmas here
    Transcending translation's sway.

You end: 'a government official hears . . .
Music and can't help dancing.' Proving he was
A strolling player once – as French professors
    And even lawyers play.

Cleaning the tit-box out this winter noon,
I think again of you. Recalling the cat
Along the summer bough that I surmised
    Might well have scared away

The parents of the peeping young, I feared
To find some gruesome corpses. But instead
I lift, on a Chelsea-bun of moss, three eggs
    From the house of doll or fay.

III

Tenners

THE SENESCHAL

The sun had long time baked the furniture,
Thrown inadvertent insects on their backs;
The myths of hangings faded to a blur.

Weeds flowered at oddish angles from the cracks
Of chimneys. In the cellars crimson wine
Turned to a rusty acid in its racks.

Yet still down passages, not a ghost, his fine
Nose raised, the seneschal of culture goes.
With his great office now he must combine

Laundering of linen, emptying of pos.

SWAN CHILDREN

How easily the sons were changed to swans!
– Almost like simply substituting letters.
And when they finally lost their avian fetters
The leathery swan-skins vanished all at once.

Miraculous! whose childhood had become
Deformed by death, step-mothers, too much love
Or lack of it. But then most men will prove
To seem quite human in the end. Though some,
Despite a whole life's effort, still stay freaks:
One of their arms a swan's wing, so to speak.

[33]

ANTIQUE SONG

I think with relief I haven't to portray
The robin's silence-breaking percussive song
That sounds far into September, into dusk,
Having already surely found a word
Somewhere in all my years to pin it down.

The old Ampico rolls I used to play,
Pedalling my Uncle Alf's pianola-grand,
They're putting on to realistic discs –
Rolling the years back, so to speak: Lhévinne's
Arpeggios immortal as the bird's.

GRAVES, 1985

Survivors from earth's remotest time –
Foxgloves and water-nymphs. The horns
Of snails are homogenous with
Their bodies, almost with their slime.
Puzzling nomenclature and myth –
Waylaying-females, monsters, Norns.

The poet Graves, amazingly
Alive, though flourishing in the Twenties,
Might well throw light on this, were he,
As once, supremely *compos mentis.*

Note: Written before Graves's death on 7 December 1985.

LONDON NIGHTS

'Lugubrious and brutal scenes' – Verlaine,
Reviewing Arthur Symons' *London Nights*.
What would those two have said, I speculate,
Set down in 1985's Soho.

Not that I often take the West End train
From these six-miles-away suburban heights
Where the worst threats to order are chocolate-
Bar wrappers on the pavement, or video-

Recorder thefts by truant boys in quiet
Hours, from houses where the rose runs riot.

AMATORY DREAMING IN OLD AGE

I dream you've left me. And what can bring you back?
For I am as I am; you as you were –
I've nothing to offer beauty, not even rape.
My heart, my entire being's sick, for there's
No chance time or the world will change my lot.

I wake, and wonder if phantom vanishing still
Implies my jealousy (at some suave god
Handling the tender flesh I thought I owned)
Or, worse, prefigures death, the final wound
Inflicted by the capricious female will.

[35]

SPOIL

It may well be the nomads have to die,
For even to gather honey they break the hive.
Yet birds, whose individual deaths we mourn,
Are just as prodigal with food that's thrown,
Although preceding us, and likely to
Outlast our doom. And having bought a few
Shares in a company that pumps out oil,
I can't help feeling guilty (in between
Checking the price and banking the dividends)
At even so humbly partaking in despoil.

VARIATIONS

The ice-compartment blindly copies nature.
I play a beheaded tape of variations,
And try to guess the composer and the theme.

On waking, I think I must and shall recall
A brilliantly clever and horrendous dream.
But what ensues? Some logical speculations

About piano trios; a fading picture
Of frightening statues made of pitch; a ball
Of ice re-charging a quarter-inch of scotch;

And further triads of essential bosh.

BEFORE THE YEAR'S TURNING

To peck the invisible leavings of the tits,
Arrives the assiduous dunnock on the snow.
Long weeks must pass before one can expect
The year to turn to better things, I know.

To alter climates, keep the crocus that
Purplish, in sheltered quarters, I found before
The snow so suddenly descended, how
Desirable! And yet who would implore

The calendar to relinquish whiteness blotted
With green, and singularly sepia-dotted?

AT THE VEGETABLE COUNTER

From Cyprus, *pommes de terre* not *pommes d'amour* –
Deep winter, our own murphies past their best.
But these are thin-skinned as the goddess, tanned
Lightly, as she, too, in that sunshine must
Have been, and powdered appropriately with sand.

Agèd, I've come to relish more and more
The simple spud, provided of decent breed –
Boiled in its jacket, preferably; hot or cold.
A poet shipped it first, with that smouldering weed
I've given up; as Venus does the old.

IN DEPTH OF WINTER

A parallel with illness and coming death,
Much disconcerting one of settled ways –
In depth of winter the central-heating fails.

The suddenness and inconvenience –
Yet not quite suddenness, for minor groans,
Slight fallings-off, were noted some time before.

And rather more than inconvenience, since
What is there left to anticipate, except
A lower level of life; great botheration;

Incompetent repairers; eternal cold?

OLD POETS

Reading old Arthur Symons in the night,
I wake and find the garden black and white;
The sky, as he might say,
A symphony of grey –
With drums of black and piccolo of white.

In the lane later, a maiden and her hind
(Leisurely playful even in the wind
That scurries the tree-top snows
And taps my old man's nose)
Leave two nigrescent trails that cross and wind.

THE MODERNIST MOVEMENT

As though to my species' infancy, I look
Out of the window on the garden wall
Whose snow-crust top a fox proceeds along
With infinite suspicion, and so prolongs
Its passion to assuage its famishment.

And then of course I go back to my book,
Founded on food and furless warmth for all
Of history. No wonder foxes' tongues
Make hideous the nights. But that man's song
Now copies them is quite a new event.

IV

Seasons

NEW YEAR'S EVE: MIDNIGHT

And so I'm to survive
Nineteen eighty-five.
Up from the river float
Sirens of the boats
To an old man's ears
Where the century's years
Throb and throb so deep
As to deny him sleep –
Though that will come anon
Now 'eighty-five has gone.

SOMETHING OF LIFE

Making to draw the curtains on the west,
I think the twilight can yield nothing more
Than bird's egg sky and clouds from some bird's breast;
And then what had been hidden in the frame
Reveals itself – the darkening's lucent core –
The planet given the goddess's name;
Mere crescent, but perfected by the eyes.

This wintry day, because the sun emerged,
So, too, the random molecules of flies.
And I held ready, when hot water surged,
A sachet of 'Foaming Bath Gel, Damask Rose'.
As James said of the notebook habit: 'To catch
And keep something of life – that's what I mean.'
Now in the curtained room, excited, clean,
I try my best with poetry to match
Everyday's marvellous and varied prose.

JOURNEY TO THE BIN

Lingering unease in moments of happiness
– Feature of old age. Out to the bin:
Full misty moon; cold February; fear.
I scuttle back indoors; perhaps already
Defences are lowered to thoracic germs.

– Back to the TV showing of a film
One knows the heroine of is forty now.
Then, she was twenty four. But nonetheless
I bless the central-heating, lack of pain;
Indeed, all life's suspiciously lenient terms.

It's merely in the interests of art
I booze too much. How many potato-peelers
Have I by accident jettisoned with the peel?
It comes to me the H-bomb's strangely apt,
Matching the non-domestic universe.

PRESERVING

Making the marmalade this year, I carve
Some peel to form the initial of your name.

Perhaps you'll come across it when I'm gone,
For even in mourning mornings will go on.

So such surprise as ancient love contrives
Will change to the kind of shock that stunned our prime.

CONVALESCING IN HIS SEVENTIES

After two weeks or so in bed, at last
A time arrives when, feeling the worst is past,
I get up almost as a matter of course,
Like an old fundamentally willing horse.

And then next day I actually go outside;
Crocuses little Indian clubs no longer,
But purple tea-cups, a party perhaps for fairies.
Even my slow steps halt so I can check
Against an ideal scale some passing stranger,
And will to safety worms that cross the road.
I start to tell myself the future's stories:
In fact, what now I must call life comes back.

RESEMBLANCES

With thanks to Amory Leggatt

Is it the plane-tree seed I think is snow? –
Not quite unseasonable, after all,
At March's end. Blind Tennyson would know.

Picked up, it's brown, of course. One speculates
On its resemblances: a savage spear,
With feathered ruff; or reference to notes.

How lavish the provision, in these days
Still chill and grey! – when old men are surprised
That dawn-birds should find anything to praise.

LITERATURE IN SPRINGTIME

With thanks to John Weightman

There already, the language, outside his head,
Strictly its nominal author could not be said
To have written À la Recherche du Temps Perdu;
Nevertheless, the novel was produced
By an entity convenient to call Proust
– Or so I read in a clever book-review.

Three petals blown against the window-pane
(By breezes one might christen Housmanesque)
Adhere through colourless, colour-flushing rain;
And one assumes the blackbirds, toddling about,
Eventually will sort their genders out
– Or so I ponder, vacant at my desk.

Despite the unseasonable chill, I go
To freeze some 'winter' trousers at the cleaners.
But shall I ever walk in them through snow
Again, observing not blossom but level Venus?
By then they may have well been left behind,
Along with the language of my verse and kind.

SPRING IN OLD AGE

Another year to go before I may
Command an action-replay of the Spring,
And see the detail inattention missed,
Or marvels which too rapidly passed by.
Could well be it will prove too long to wait.
A pity one hasn't got it all on tape.

EARLY AND LATE WORKS

Beethoven and Scriabin in their late
Works became fascinated by the trill –
More reminiscent of an angled bill
Than any throbbing of a *diva*'s throat.
Though art that copies an inhuman call
Is no more strange than, say, the chestnut's frill
Of pencil-sharpenings coloured softest green
Coiled from some pencil-sharpening machine
Of Spring; leaves first to come, and first to fall.

TIT TRICKS

Tits perform disappearing tricks
With the minute-holed nesting box.
What other reason can there be
For the astounding frequency
Except the poet's rhymed applause?
Since surely merely natural laws
Cannot compel the weary wills,
However many tiny bills.

GARDEN QUERIES

9.25: the throstle's resourceful song
Goes on. To whom or what, is the question raised.

Later, the garden's silent in the night,
A crescent moon aloft. And equally

One speculates as to inherent wrong
In the cosmos. When that initial atom blazed

How could the mystery of reflected light
Have been foreseen, after dusk's melody?

WEEDING IN SUMMER

It must have been a robin I saw alight.
Beside the trowel a single petal fell
From an orange-blossomed rose just in my sight.
It must have been a robin I saw alight:
Colour and side-slipping motion both were right.
So even peripherally I could tell
It must have been a robin I saw alight
Beside the trowel. A single petal fell.

PERCEPTION

Child with lashes like moths, and ash-blonde hair,
We only too easily predict your fate:
Inevitable change to dark from fair.

The blackbird with his gold-rimmed spectacles
Sees through the dusk to cluck a warning, though
Possibly of unspecific ills.

But a worse destiny is never to grow
To vandyke. As is a universe through human
Folly no kind of eye can ever know.

GREAT EVENTS

When merely-to-be embraces everything –
Or, rather, just before that sessile time –
Is the time of happiness I'm nearly at.

Already joy is almost always in
The air. Through garden dusk moths lead me on
As Ariel the conspiritors. Ahead,

The room is lit, the vermouth's oil revolves
Beneath the ice according to some law
That might rule daring currents in the mind.

The destiny of poets is not to age;
Although a few grow old. Damn it, I'll not
Enshed the garden-chairs; thus engineer

Tomorrow's great event – the shock of meeting
Light-fleeing earwigs when I come to unfold
The blue or scarlet in yet another noon.

JULY

To hear the wind softly in the trees, yet fail
To feel it on one's face – a test for summer.
I carry a tea-tray to our (so-called) terrace:
Peanut-butter or *patum peperium*;
A freshly-out *London Mag* or *Private Eye*;
A dish of soaked crusts for my pals the birds.
A set of pleasures rather close to guilt.

Already children are playing in the lane –
The start of their enormous evening,
Through which the various birds will go on singing.

But I come in and mix a drink, and sit
To write a verse or two, and see along
The ceiling rivers and railway-lines of light –
The falling sun reflected from points of silver,
Even my watch-glass, soon to disappear
In favour of a white door's shadow-play,
Globules the apple's myriad leaves admit
As though foreshadowing the fruit to come.

July's more transient than children's games,
Themselves untypical of the human lot
As happiness. Yet even in old age
Time sometimes lingers on a fabulous page.

FRUIT-TREE

The apparatus draws up rain
Whence it emerges once again
Packaged conveniently within
A bright impermeable skin,
Nonetheless edible, although
Old teeth and tongues mayn't find it so.
But what could resemble a machine
Less than a shapeless tower of green,
Dropping around at random these
Botched products of its processes?
– Which some fastidious birds ignore,
Thieving inside the factory store.

TEA-TIME

Upon a methylated thistle-head
A blurred brown butterfly. Sun after rain;
A sudden heat; smell of near rottenness
From lofty grass. Returning from the lane,

I see the legs of sparrows pink against
The sun. The usual Coleridgean tone.
I think: have the malignant times worked simply
In my case to make a lifetime's work unknown?

A lady sparrow's nibbling beak removes
The surface of my bread and butter. Hell!
Birds eating danegeld at a quid per mere
Five hundred grams. Yes, that's the age as well.

IMAGES

With thanks to Paul Jacobs

'The moon falls on some temple that has been' –
Translation that would risk Debussy's scorn,
He having changed the title so it made
A perfect alexandrine; the piece itself
Crumbled yet sparkling, with elusive tune.

Peacocks imitate harps, and *vice-versa*.
An idiot adolescent with his mother,
Still holding hands; perhaps a compensation,
After fifteen or so unchanging years.
Behind, a sky the colour of girls' dresses.

I glimpse a phrase that makes the short-hairs rise:
'The ruined library of Zanzibar.'
Bonfire smoke drifting, sun through leaves, and slant
White-vapoured shafts. Beneath a photograph,
A caption: 'Bubble Chamber Arabesques.'

With CO_2 my scotch is interfused:
Apparently not miracle enough
To drink a hydrogen and oxygen
Commixture. Rather brings to mind the *image*
That adds the great crowning from *Boris Godunov*.

The creeper knows when it must start to blush.
As in a 'magic' painting-book, the hose
Reveals an unsuspected spider's web.
Summer's about to end: let's hope to be
Inspired by rotten weather, like Debussy.

OLD PUZZLES

Past colleagues at a funeral: I greet
Such spouses as turn up; moreover, am
Myself one who must render thanks the lame,

The pale, the grey, the wrinkled, still endure.
But those who arrive alone – do I enquire
After their dearest? Perhaps who're dead, or dying;

Perhaps whose fate I really know, for now
I can as easily forget the worst
As specs, or tea or turnips on a list.

Are we the last in an epoch of divorce
And sleeping round to bring our ancient passion
To rituals where love is interred or burnt?

I see a dead worm on the churchyard stone,
Dried out in the Indian summer, looking like
Half that old puzzle of the tangled nails.

But everywhere the mysterious couples with
The commonplace: each gossiping mourner must
Lie down unwilled in a capsule quite alone.

SURVIVORS

I

Old fly, November fly,
Survivor of the summer,
I'll miss you in the kitchen
Where you investigate
Even such famine regions
As the spatula handle
– Though you've lived on so long
(Nights of frost-brilliant moons,
Mornings of running panes),
Missing me's more the question.

II

Kitchen fly, bedroom fly,
Why don't you get together,
In this pre-winter weather?
Perhaps you're one and the same –
Unverifiable surmise;
Observer-and-observed
Part of the quantum theory;
And so because of the very
Nature of the universe
Condemned to loneliness.

WARD 1G

I

October's end: a glow of sun by day,
And carmine dusks; and moths adhering to
Night-blackened windows – leniencies to match

Your scaffold-timed reprieve, that's also mine.
Even a crew of wasps comes out to take
A final sip of *nouveau* apple-juice,

Bask in residual warmth. Against the light,
The gossamer rigging of a ghostly barque –
Even of fairy complement – is glimpsed.

The apple leaves are dry beneath the tree;
A butterfly settles like a medal on
My breast – a bassoon emerging from the *tutti*.

The setting moon is half a lemon slice
Of dubious imitation sweetmeat fruit
Among the yellower, more regular

Rilkean roadway chandeliers. And what
Than lingering roses in the sodium glare
Can seem more ambiguous in their physique?

I must instruct the video to record
A programme, while I visit you in Ward
1G: a similar device enshrines

The time set by providence for our demise;
Although I can die happy, as it were,
Now you've revived the cliché that life would lack

Meaning without you. Constantly forgotten,
The lesson's re-taught – fear not, crunch away:
The apple-grub is mostly made of apple.

II

The foyer of the district hospital,
The corridors, the wards themselves, confirm
The gulf between the *condition humaine*

And contemplative life, as though one yet again
Were being called on, contrary to desire,
To serve the armed nation, a will outside oneself.

Noting the plaster that attaches you
To various tubes, I wonder what's secured
By a finger's band – and see your wedding-ring.

III

Then it's the time when mad dogs on the heath
Loom through the darkness, followed by their masters:
Devotion by the human to the brute.

On my way home a usual cat miauls
To get my nails beneath its stropping jaw,
Flea-bitten probably; yet rewarding service.

And gratitude to enigmatic powers,
Malevolent on the whole, wells up as I
Return to music's marvels, while you lie

Rather too closely still to the realms of Dis.